THE ME

Karen Eberhardt Shelton

and

Jay Ramsay

DAVID
PAUL

Published by David Paul, 2002

29 Redston Road
London N8 7HL
Tel. 020 8347 9857
http//:www.davidpaulbooks.com

ISBN 0-9540542-1-0

Set in 10 on 14 point Caslon 540 Roman

Cover design by Thomas R. Izzard
Text design and typesetting by Will Shaman

Printed in England by Antony Rowe Ltd

CONTENTS

Acknowledgements

The quote from David Gascoyne's poem for radio (who died while this book was in progress) is from *Collected Poems* (Oxford University Press, first published 1965).

We are grateful to the editors of the following magazines in which some of these poems first appeared:

Terrible Work, Envoi, New Humanity, The Word, Caduceus, Phoenix New Life Poetry, Tears in the Fence, Rebirth, Seventh Sense, Blue Moon Rising and *Network Ireland*.

'Nakedness' appeared in *Meditations on the Unknown God* (University of Salzburg, 1996); 'Kosovo' in *Voices for Kosovo* ed. Rupert Loydell (Stride, 1999); 'La Maison de Dieu' in *The World Book of Healing* and 'Anytown Stroud: to You' in *The Book of Hope* ed. Birgitta Jonsdottir (*Beyond Borders*, Reykavik, Iceland, 2002), both launched in New York. The complete 'After Rumi' sequence by Jay Ramsay is published by The Lotus Foundation (www.lotusfoundation.org.uk).

The Tower cover image taken from a classic French tarot pack.
Meaning: Unforeseen catastrophe; disruption of one's style of life or way of thinking, which may be followed by enlightenment.

Preface

WE ARE two poets – one originally from America, the other England – united in the belief that poetry can help rekindle a vital flame at this critical time. For 5 years, Karen was an associate editor of California's *Green Fuse* poetry magazine, while Jay co-founded *Angels of Fire* in London during the mid-80's, and in the years since, both have used poetic license to confront the ethical and spiritual lapses that colour our impact on the world.

We met in the year 2000 while reading at the Wessex International Poetry Festival in Blandford Forum, Dorset, where we were drawn together by a recognition of shared values and similar outlooks – where the kinship that developed would support us through the trials of a country ravaged by foot and mouth and that unbelievable yet real cataclysmic smoke-filled blue morning in New York – September 11, 2001 – the collapse of the twin towers and subsequent acts of retribution. Violence upon violence. A hardening of hearts that has cast a dark shadow over all creation.

W.H. Auden stated, "Poetry that is news, stays news." As poets, we believe poetry has the power to reflect 'news' of past and present, to send bulletins of consciousness, dispatches of awareness. As poets, we assimilate and record blunders and atrocities of history that have been veiled in silence, secrecy and complacency. We wait and watch, hope, worry, wonder – and continually struggle to interpret the shifting currents that carry us onward.

We employ poetry to focus our understanding, provide us with imaginative and strong eyes to *read the world*, and help us progress beyond rhetoric, patriotism, rationalization, and polarized points of view; to prod our hearts to confront the messy realities that ripple through all levels of society, everywhere. No matter how thick the rain of arrows, ultimately, our longing to celebrate one caring humanity, calls us to bear witness as trustworthy custodians and lovers of life. The message is clear – we are just two of its messengers.

KAREN EBERHARDT SHELTON

Karen was raised in California where she was associate editor of *Green Fuse* poetry magazine for five years. Her first book of poetry, *Two Sisters* was published in the States. Her poems have appeared in anthologies (*Cartwheels on the Faultline*, *Saltwater/Sweetwater*) and in collections all over the world, as have many essays and travel articles. For three years she was a columnist for *The Western Daily Press*.

Karen is also an established photographer and has held two photographic exhibitions.

For Jean Schulz in California, Michael Hunter in London and David Barker of New Zealand – significant helpers, inspirers. My mother and father, foot servants of "redundant angels" – each showing up when the wolf howled.

Open-mindedness is a quality that will always exist where the desire for knowledge is genuine. Bertrand Russell

"Come to the edge", he said. "We're afraid", they said. But they came; he pushed them, and they flew. Apollinaire

A Modern Agenda

Dear God of the green satin
Oh roof above me listening
The tears in dry grasses opening –
How well it is designed, the fruit
And the listening, the weeping, a voice
In the orchard heavy-breasted, oh
Everyone, all of you, your mandate

Is here with these shadows drifting
Around us after the flowering
Of another day – there is a will
That can't be commanded – a trust
From the beginning, a lift from beyond
In this sorrow for running away.

How well to be grounded under rooftops
A hint of significance, something
That plays with the way things are
And messes fondly with the vagaries of heart.

FEAR

Sometimes at night
When we all lie down together
Whether it be under wood or leaf
Or the cover of a house,
Each in our own way sleeping,
It seems something in the dark
Or beyond the dark – the farthest
Thing which we know and beyond that,
The merely suspected, unnameable
Might come for us,
Take us singly or in pairs or groups
Away, beyond where we sleep,
How we are named,
What we are,
And shatter us.

Feeling our smallness
Against the unknown
Despite the familiar walls
Of the room, the old fence,
The usual things in their usual places
The dark holds a pulse
Not our own.
It breathes inaudibly
Outside the window,
Within the shadows of trees,
Around our bodies,
Slipping among the hours
In prickly, tangible waves,
Making daylight our only escape.

The Solace I Long To Come By

I want to lay my problems at somebody's feet
Not to give them away
But to feel less weight from them
To simply breathe again through my nose
To sleep through one whole night
Like a baby on clean cotton sheets
To hear my girl's phone call from America
And realize it wasn't made
Because she took too many pills

To walk away from artificial lights
To be somewhere small and easy and intelligent
To be still and struck when a butterfly alights on the newspaper
Wings so painted with Egyptian and circles of red sun
You can't believe she exists
And then be different and sleep in grass on a whim
The fables of other rhythms at work
In the quizzical blood of hope

When luminous light after rain erupts
I want to creep into a courgette's yellow trumpet
And tap the moist walls,
Living tissue on the ground
Tied to the earth by a root

Where are my roots?
Cells in my feet twitching when I arrive
Where there are no houses side by side
A horse neighing, thunder
A sense of belonging without arbitrary ties

The long afternoon exhales an inclusive lullaby;
I want the rest to go away and stop being artificial
Merely croon in context with the sliding hours
Like before we came foundering and reordering
Bent on the paradox of destroying as the way to a better life

I want the long rivulets of coursing wet
To remove scars, erase disease
Soothe foxgloves in the walls where they bow and scrape
Cajole doves and blackbirds to keep being what they are

I want to slide between their private mysteries
And the shattering parasites of my own kind
Without sacrificing even one object of natural intent

Tough Young Men

The young men who smoke, drink and cry *fuck you*
Are everywhere.
Their stony faces glance a quarter turn to the left
When they drive past a facet of sorrow;
A sparrow wobbling,
A lame turkey,
Silly girls strolling close to the pavement edge.

They stare straight through me
Tattoos blue on their bare brown skin
Chins up, lips set
Into locked ramparts,
Windowless towers,
Cages whose constraints
They have no knowledge of.

These tough young men
Who try to be manly
Behave as if cocks
Were locks
Barring their chemistry
From showing a soft anomaly
That would, if revealed,
Undress what is *actually* underneath;
Like maybe a baby's belly
Or a heart that would crack if dropped.

It takes so little for them to bomb something
Or hedge praise.
They go there knowing nothing,
No idea who they are.
They are lusting for action, a plume of smoke
Rising from their mouths.
They will do almost anything
To be noticed,
Even if you hate them for having to stare
At the mess of their lives.

But they too are sacred;
One has to dig beneath the bitter shell.

WHERE WERE YOU? HOW COULD YOU?

What if no one cares about you,
Pays no attention?
What if you're a fence post
And everyone sits on you
Or you're a yellow line
And the world drives over you?
Or you sing and everyone is surprised?
What happens if no one thinks about you
Or asks how you feel?
What if you're a rainbow
And no one looks up?

What if there's a need to say something
About what's tearing you apart
And they hang up without answering?
Who will listen with you to the murmur
You hear deep inside the ground,
Like a severed artery
Bleeding to death?

What if you and the earth
Are the same plasma
The same heartbeat
Counting the stabbings and reckless thirst
And no one questions how this can be?

What if you stop imploring
And no one notices you have gone
And trees march toward the desert one by one?

"So we all stand up and act sad, and then what do we do? If you're cremated, you don't go to heaven, because there's no body left to go. How can flies and worms get in if the coffin is shut? And if they can't get in, how can they eat the body? When you think about it, it's scary if dead bodies are left lying under the ground for ever and ever."

Remarks of a young person after a funeral service.

DEPARTURES

For Ken, whom my sister loved very much.

Death comes along so many roads:
To the wild turkey strutting across at dawn,
To the running deer assaulted by a car.
It will come later for the black vultures ripping at her,
A flurry of them rising and riding the air, waiting.
To the small worm, a dry pink crescent.
To the snake, flattened into tape.
To the shiny leather of what was once a body.

The end is in the dead Styrofoam,
The plastic carton,
The cigarette butt,
The nylon rag
Draining life-blood from the earth
While all the other dead are giving it back.
We, the still-living, stand up for them
As they return to the ground to start over,
To dream again about what they will become.

A man takes his quota of things,
Leaving sometimes when there is still some left;
Not needing all of it now,
Returning in small ways as a reminder
He will be come back over and over;
Maybe as Ken, maybe as someone else.
He knows now he is eternal.
In our own ways when the time comes
We will learn about this too.

LARRY IN THE ADIRONDACKS

He went east to the Adirondacks,
A quest of the wilderness for a week. He tried
Fishing but read a book about weeping elephants
And couldn't cast a hook. He scored the surface in a canoe,
Hunter on a bed of hyacinths,
The star spangled man learning to watch
Firelight, water weight,
Slow pearls of a beaver's thought
Moored beside the transparent edge of shore,
Receivers and transmitters both trying to grasp their proximities.
Light and shade becoming one cathedral
As if for his pleasure something beyond him,
Something only the pond knew to ensnare him
In a galaxy of fireflies, rippled fish, silence, a walled green world.

Wearing nothing but shorts, he laid down the paddle,
Sat transfixed in warm summer beads pocking the surface
Around him, melting softly into the lake
Beside the faint whisper of opening lily pad flowers
In voices strangely their own.
Water above and below baptising, rinsing
Man-part-fish-part-spirit, waterweed, mirror.

That night he watched the beacons of fireflies working
Air and water, on and off, their cool fire
As amazing as anything he'd seen in his whole life.

The power of warm summer rain on his bare body
As if for his pleasure, dissolving him into the scene, holistic
And primeval, sensuality too pristine for mockery,
Luminous canopy floating cloud-like over the pond,
Silent reflection, the merging of creation and the ideal;
Deep and silver, spun into mist that sighs and breathes.

ON THE CUTTING OF OLD-GROWTH REDWOODS

Decapitations in the Garcia river watershed –
The great throats slit
The earth booming like a drum when the heads fall
Soft red corpses chained down by pall bearers
That hurtle along the coast
With steel frames and burly engines
And quotas indifferently stamped on them;
Moist shafts bucking the west wind
With 500 and 1,000 years
Of memory and history and primordial silence
Lying dead within
Mere board feet and sawdust
Giants rendered into pygmies
Stacked in suburban lumber yards
Their assassins air conditioned at the bank
Lunching with clones of corporate vanity
Beyond the reach of marbled murrelets
Beyond conscience for their breach of faith
With the earth's intent;
Strangers to this rare, damp-loving breed.
Only on this Pacific coast
Only here mixed with fog
And sylvan mystery do these vast stalks erupt
To outlast all projections
And mortal spans.
Favoured, fragrant, matchless, slain
Destined by commerce
To submit to the fate of mere trees.
These big ones beseech us:
Speak for them.
Allow them 500 more years, extra eons
The completion of their natural span.
Believe they will whisper all history
When human decay returns to earth.

Cow rumps swishing past the loose arms of oaks
Rabbits wandering through yellow broom
Soprano hawks' blue-edged flutey love songs
Stems and twigs pushing out their thickened buds
Grass swelling in a great pulsation of tenderness
These partners humming the elegant notes of spring

Then it is fog again and the drift of it comes down;
She walks in white, weeping for all the damaged things
Her experienced heart as filled with energy
As the scented imperative performing in the tangled vetch;
Live cleanly, drop the lies, convert the indifferent fringe
Respond to even the most demanding convolutions of life

She thinks of opponents with legitimate arguments
Warms to those who live in scale with reason and common sense
Wishes the well intentioned would never suffer

Would you abandon your place for the sake of your furniture
The things in your sphere that are lightweight?
There is a natural price attached to everything
To be counted maybe next spring or even long after
Though the robins are singing to you now
Amongst these willowy matings of beautiful bodies
Profusely extolling each layer of the process
With sheer unprogrammed extravagance
Of unlimited free offerings

My soprano, your tenor, hyacinth, spumed waves' arch
Swallows that return over and over against the odds
Migrating monarchs and terns, things still unknown;
How foolish those immune to the flux of the greatest power.
I know not one poet or artist or musician who can encompass it
Not one deep soul able to resist or stand apart

Not My Africa

If you lived in Uganda, Zaire –
Walking to the water pump
Three times a day

One spare dress

A lamp, a plate, a single book

Coped with the sticks and bones
And outstretched skin
Of your own little Charles or Andrew

What you do would be infused
With proportion and relevance
As though living

Was a conscious thing

After all.

The U.S. serviceman who bombed kids with napalm during the Vietnam war, eventually met with the grown Vietnamese woman who was the naked, fleeing, scorched child captured in a photo at the time, a photo that went round the world. The sequel to that episode went round the world too.

MAKING AMENDS

He has closed her horrified mouth
With a kiss of apology,
His own suffering
A bridge between them.

He is a rare gift:
To heal with an embrace
So many years after burning off her flesh
In a hateful war;
Having forgiveness come back to him
Was the closure of a century

That she survived to face him,
That he lived to grow into compassion;
One of those perfect miracles
You can't explain, yet it is so beautiful,
It illuminates everyone.

THE REAL KILLERS

Dupont, instead of *just* making money
Couldn't you disdain your shareholders for once
And be gleefully environmental?
I.C.I., have you never marked a shooting star
And shivered with knowledge of your own mortality?

Is that *ALL* men can do on earth – grow rich?
If *He* weighs the energy of all fading super nova,
How can Mr. Moneybags turn his back
On the enormity of life's basic lessons?
Liar, predator, extortionist –
Mean little men with titles who don't hesitate
To sign contracts that translate into death
By consolidation, merger, acquisition,
Extinction by profit and poisoned ledgers.

It's true, so why can't I say it?
Wealth suffocates, deadens, blinds, and oh yes,
It mostly corrupts. I've looked into the eyes
Of millionaires and CEO's and seen
How they're blinded and how the imprint
Of inconsequential things on their retinas –
Objects like stoats and lichens, cumulus clouds –
Stops in the back of their sockets
And never reaches the heart of the brain.

That is why they're unaware of true wealth
And where it originates, how it lives, why it dies.
They want oil beneath the tundra
And care nothing for the caribou walking above.
You overlook the timeless value of lifeblood,
You silly men in suits…

Ritual Feast (Ode to Thanksgiving)

There was smog to the east from this viewpoint
Or maybe the smoke of a burned turkey.
Our dog watered a fencepost, carried slobber on his chin
Stupid gunshot in the country hills
Sherry and wrinkled apples.
What now? The turkey roaster and potatoes
Won't fit in one oven.
Oh football! Damp clothes sagging on the line.
Chilly sun and mauve chrysanthemum
Behold the bed with fresh flannel sheets.
Politics repeat in the headline's national blunders
Unlike the Puritans and Indians
Forging first links over baked squash
As primeval gratitude linked their hearts
With a clear joy at coming so far.
Hail to touchdowns and microwaves
These big brothers guiding the character of our thanks.
The papers were fat with ads today
The nation spends well to earn its rosy plums
And encouragement from Talking Bears and Robots
That suck out the dumb portions of its purse
The remainder of earth's storehouse
Interacts as usual, uncomplaining and wise
And obeys the genetic summons to cooperate
And be one.

Poor women, basting their birds
Testing cranberries for tart sweetness
And pinching the crusts of pies, nationwide
Ignoring twinges of tiredness
And suppressed revolt.
Thanksgiving wears on their bones
And they know it wasn't always such a test as this.
Men in the clearings fire up their chainsaws
Sweat over sawdust as they wait for meat
And another fabled story to be written at home.
The earth sees its death descending
During this most ambiguous feast;
Like an ending, deceit prevails
And with grave apathy we eat.

Fecund Folly

A Saudi newspaper reports
That the wife of Abdullah Mohammed Ali
Is going home from the hospital with seven new babies,
Home to six other children already born;
When will he have time for two other wives and nine more kids?

I do the arithmetic; in his fifty five years,
One man has produced as much as a rabbit or guinea pig
And I wonder if there's a good reason for this.
How will thirteen children play in a two-bedroom house?
Will they stand four abreast around the toilet?
Eat in shifts? One spoon passed along?
Thirteen toothbrushes,
Thirteen sets of sandals by the door?

How do they wash the clothes?
Thirteen kids is half the class, too many for one car.
The family at one table would fill the room,
The doctor's office, the library, the grocery store.

Each will eventually want to work,
Have a home. They will marry, have families of their own,
Populate the suburbs with chairs, laundry, bicycles
Their waste, excess, leavings, bins of plastic, grease
And that is how we live, packing them in
To Planet Stadium until the bleachers are a dark sea of faces
And every snail and beetle has been trampled beneath a glut of feet.

THE SHIMMER THAT YOU RECOGNIZE

Some of the best parts of life
Come on wings
A couple of perfect lines in a book
Capturing an ideal
The eagle of a brilliant idea
Mention somewhere on lips or paper
That one person exceeded the commonplace
Offered hope
A bar of light
An uplifting ripple
Like the catch in the throat
When a large bird swoops low
And that rustle of taffeta
Beats in your ear
Urging you to quicken

The lift comes from anywhere
Suddenly
Faster blood, spiritual recognition
The full-blown urgent reminder
Not to give in
To second best
The dull mire of soured expectations

Go only with the elation
Of here, I have found you!
Oh, I hear what you are saying
Wondrous ideal and deeds
As perfect as the eagle's hollow wing

How Do You Want To Be Remembered?

As a little puff of firecracker on the 4th of July
A thick-armed tree cutter in virgin forest
A series of selfish fence lines

Someone who drives too fast down the hill
And uses money only as money
A body, a pair of breasts, come-hither flesh

A woman who finally retired after 40 years
The neighbour who zaps insects, shoots your dog
A father who never signed one letter: *'Love, Dad'*.

Remembered for being invisible, derelict, indifferent?
Or stopping to help when there's a need
Alert mind, dull mind, the sleeping tool

Or one who looks around to see that all is well
Who trembles in the details of excess
Whose heart flutters on hearing something beautiful

So many poems seem to have come from the sequins of repressed light, the blue light of a half-awake soul, a root pushing up through the dense soil of longing, striving, a yearning to break through to the ground where things are named, understood, comforting. . .

WHAT IS SHE, REALLY?

Sometimes that's all there is
During the passing

Of twilight, after work, later
The rusk of cat on couch

One CD being played over and over;
The clock, even with battery, ticks. Memory.

A hollow kind of hour, halting, thin-skinned,
Thick with the lisp of habit
Saying more of the same over and over.

That's Venus above, a lovely light
To encourage these borders stretching,
A shimmer on the edge of repression,

One affable touch
Of all she imagines,
Blue veins in the kingdom of night,

Not strangers, merely the way
Stars come down.

The breath of pine
Each time she opens the door

And begins again, over and over.

INVESTING TIME

The day ends
And leaves you stranded somewhere;
On a back road maybe
Or your own home
The strange convolutions of your mind.

And there you are
While a tiny hummingbird stares in the window
Shadows throw ink over the land
Clouds drift toward the Sierra

And it is now
You must assess
Your giving, taking, everything wasted
While you squandered the hours

Eternity creeps up
Your crop of numbers shrinks down;
The arrival of a new sunset and another and another;
Surely you can find reason to prioritize

Oh pleasant day, so easily dribbled
Away in the warm hummingbird hours
Honeysuckle's perfume creeping over the deck

The languid growing
Like amnesia infiltrating all that needs doing;
So easy to forget that whole lifetimes are spent on nothing.

LIFE IS A DANGEROUS PLACE

To Alyson Hallett

The farm woman said *fresh eggs*
But I boiled them and the shells peeled off easily
Which means those eggs had been sitting around.
People talk about things that aren't real
As though *experts* know things I don't

I drive southward through rain
On back roads where I know nothing
Except to follow the thread between hedgerows
Faintly suspecting they will lead me to think

I've been somewhere.
Yet farms resting on green pillows
Have lives of their own; orbits, cycles, personal mud
And I realize we're all guardians of our own artefacts.

After meeting with a poet in a country pub
The way leads past two lakes and wild ducks
Though I have no idea where I am
As though my exploration of that poet's soul
Has usurped my usual map

How can there be an answer
When so many questions fly in like crows
Landing to devour the planted seeds,
As though I'd learned something from the poet
But didn't know where to keep it on the way home

As with the other arrows that shoot in;
Cows and pigs and sheep with blistered lips,
All of Europe with closed shutters;
Regret after thinking one could just smile and eat
And knowing it's nothing like that.

These serious times filled with death and losses,
The souls of mournful sheep usurped by fire.
I am home now, parched with confusion,
As though going into so-called ordinary space
Was no longer a journey I could bear to make

CHOPIN'S WEATHER

Chopin's passion stands out during the fog's quiet hymn
A piano of the heart
Like enflamed oratory as this chill surges in
You function in what is regular, how you've built it
Around you, routine allowing the formations
To exist, harmonize, continue
As if you were satisfied and there it is –
Your life managing to be.

Then Chopin intervenes on a blurry night
Rapture and rupture
Bringing another century to life
On the keyboard so you can feel him then
Reaching for the same things
That torment us near the century's end

His touch on the black and white keys
Is like history
A statement, an attitude
Playing to his friends, his lovers
His dirty underwear, the stupid way men
Misinterpret everything important

The sallies of heart into sunflowers
And Polish springs and the way she kissed
His thumb as he played repeatedly
The things that spoke to him
Like wheat and lamplight
Shutters banging in the wind
A glove beside the candle
His fervour exploding on the keyboard

SOLSTICE

We're all starved for light.
The house becomes a starship,
Probing illuminations in trees
Down ravines
All along the fence
The edges of the barn
On every angle of a person's face.
Where we eat, a tiny string of bulbs
In the living room, against the front wall.
Candles on the table
And window ledges, in the kitchen
By the stove, reflected in glass.

Even the planted things grow;
Persimmons like suns
Cranberries' maroon fire
Crimson shocking in poinsettias
The green thunder of holly's gloss

We drive by watching, sucked in, consumed
A majority still desensitised.
Some, who bludgeon little dogs to death
Overkill whatever they touch
Rip layers apart wherever they go
Prey in the dark – grope, defile
Never see brilliance in ordinary matter

There is a desperate need for light,
For listening to Bach's oratorio
Wading in the phosphorescence of sea
Waking in the crystal of the White Mountains
Going where the line folds
And meets in a blending
Of the darkest night
And the first new minute of day

Written after watching a TV movie depicting the events of January, 1972 on Bloody Sunday in Ireland, when paratroopers shot dead 13 unarmed civilians and wounded a further 15 during an illegal civil rights march in Derry, Northern Ireland.

WHEN I LOOK UP AT THE STARS

Walked out last night into the moonlessness
Dog running free into shadows and weeds
I found Andromeda, Orion, the Bear, North Star, the Dipper
And circling with them swarms of relatives
Transmitting their torches for at least 50 billion years

Uncountable, both the stars and the years
That inconceivable, mega-bulbed canvas in space
Hard-wired to the eon's store
Body of the universe spilling into my heart

I gaped heavenward dizzy and dumbstruck
Held by a cold black cavernous incentive to *think*
The Looking Up, the canopy beyond words
Derided as it were by imposter flares
Plugged in to a cloud-wreathed keening earth

A toad leapt then in the starlight
Water gushed in sparkles down the streambed
I heard a faint sighing in the airwaves
Lanterns kept arriving from time beyond my scope

And theirs, the broken, hungry, quarrelling lands
Where light is missing; there's a glue not formed
Dull eyes are not learning to look beyond and know

How calmly simple to breathe the stars
To worship in the garden flaring above the ground
To reap the outcome if others do the same

A BIG BANG FOR THE MONEY

When I read poetry
An aching column of desire
Rises in me and meets
With everything the world is

Poets make me want to know about life
The inexhaustible, inexpressible, ineffable
Mornings after wet nights;
Wind, coffee, the last day of October
Ocean swells ridden by sea birds
A sentence that captures the truth
Caribou running over tundra

And that is just the beginning;
They will *be* wherever there is a pulse
Divining purpose, sentiment
The lost offers of prosperity and love
What moves the snail
Hidden light

Like explorers in small boats
Following the swells of particularness
Identity, naming things that are naked
Their minds staking our paradise
And the slum
Ecstasy, conundrums, the failed start
On the mystery of words

How I love everything they offer
As though I were sand
And they kept pouring liquid
Into my yearning pores

NONE IS WITHOUT THE OTHER

I hear the stars fall
I hear the owls hoot
I hear the water talk
I hear the frog's chorus
I hear fox feet break the leaves
I hear rocks click under hooves
I hear tigers prowling
I hear fire cracking in the trees
I hear branches break
I hear bears snuffle
I hear a humming bird faster than I can see
I hear the tenors of whales
I hear everything, being a mother
Guarding the whimper before time formed,
In my cave.

I know the whispers, the footfalls
The shrieks and the dying
The sigh of the petal unfolding

I am here in the world as it really is
As it forms itself
As it stays connected
As it remembers always how to return.

Stop this, and the code is ripped
Then broken. The wolves founder
There is no heartbeat to answer the howl.

THREE THINGS

Because they are *all* dying, I should walk by *one*
That's pitifully crying out?
Ignore the universal language of prehistory?

A lamb in a far field, over and over.
I would have gone and found it
Ripped my clothes on wire, broken the law
To do what I could for that solitary bleat

Where should I look for the real world?
It is not here in this foolishness, these detached lives
All these noisy people driving cars
Making bland excuses for the extravagance of death.
I want to be somewhere that's still wild and a little free

And then I would try to be kind,
Be someone who offered and worked hard;
Not for money, but to peel back the errors,
Attach a loving stamp somewhere gritty

This oath, a promise to all that breathes;
I am here for life, not the ruthless exit.
I embrace the ewe, pig's breath,
the progeny of worms.

THE WRITTEN WORLD

Life is not just about being who you are now –
Stuck with a glass of gin,
Bulgar wheat and cabbage
The way you've always done things
The way it has always been

Realization comes, slowly
You learn bit by bit
Fundamentalist Moslems, militant Jews
Subtle forms of violence and love
Until one day you have to speak out
About how you see the world
And where the rich, confusing roll of events
Takes your soul, leaves it stranded
Elevates it to ecstasy

What do you have to say
And how will it be expressed?
You must find a way to say something
You, a new body in an ongoing world

There must be cause for reaction
A limit to spill over from
A burning in the stem

Your knowledge comes from writers
As though Tolstoy or Camus had organized
Their ideas and personally talked to you
So that you could *think* and be changed

Every writer takes its turn;
Emphatically, compellingly, over and over
Explaining the world
So that by the time each human is old
They'll have drawn in enough wisdom
To leave a compassionate legacy,
Ideas for new children to interrogate
The crux of it all to be explored.

To you, Iceland, Japan, Norway…

A Whale's Lament

I've just learned Quakers killed whales,
So I wonder about the nature of morality, conscience, theory

That assumed *license to kill*
Even her grand body gliding underwater
Like a vast shrimp

Sperm whales with brains six times larger
Than a human brain

The *Nantucket Sleigh Ride*;
The towing and torment of a whale
Until, hours later, her life is spent

And blood cascades through her blow hole,
What men called *chariots of fire*;
As though she was nothing more than undulating kelp

And they did that, over and over
As though their souls had died –
Their own, not whales'

MAKING A DIFFERENCE

If there was one mantra or sign or look
That would bring everything together;
One bite of a wild cherry,
A heart-cried-out prayer,
A life wrapped in the eventual consequence
Of clinging to principle,
The striving would take on dimension;
Like the shape of a bottle, a rug,
The colour of sheets, origins of pottery;
Clay, mould, feather, silica, design.

It's all this thinking and preparing
Without teachers; one's driver driving one
Perpetually toward a line in the sand,
A horizon, a culmination of ideals;
The loneliest of occupations, the mad heart
Pestering, echoing, repeating;
There is no other way to turn.

And still, no one listens. There is no answer
Reminding, prodding, interjecting,
Every now and then sending out a companion cry
Of anguish and supplication,
Passionate reminders that we cannot
Do all this forever without reverberation,
Without hearts breaking all around us,
Hearts that would rather give something back,
Rather beat for a purpose,
Be held as a model of the best in us,
The most sublime.

JAY RAMSAY

Jay Ramsay is a prolific and popular author and editor of poetry, prose and translations. Poetry includes *Kingdom of The Edge* (Element,1999), *Tao Te Ching* with Martin Palmer (Element/Vega reprint 2002) and *Love's Way – the alchemy of relationships*. Co-founder of the *Angels of Fire* radical poetry collective in 1983. Poetry editor of *Kindred Spirit* and project director of Chrysalis poetry courses. He is an accredited psychosynthesis therapist and NFSH spiritual healer and runs workshops worldwide.

For Donna

Voice B: A war goes on within against the shadows.
Voice D: Who speaks tonight of war and battle? Go to bed!
David Gascoyne, *Night Thoughts*

And the message today is how to die. Bob Geldof, Live Aid, July 1985

We are not the message… we are the messengers… the message is love.
Wim Wenders, from the film, *Far Away, So Close.*

PRELUDE from transmissions

XXIV

I saw a great light come down over London,
And buildings and cars and people were still
They were held wherever they were under the sky's
Clear humming radiance as it descended –
Everywhere, in shops, behind desks and on trains
Everything stopped as the stillness came down
And touched the crown of our heads
As our eyes closed, and the sky filled us
And our minds became the sky –
And everyone, regardless of crime class or creed
Was touched; as slowly we began to stir
Out of this penetrated light-filled sleep
Dizzily as the hand completed its dialling,
And the train lurched forward
And I saw faces looking at one another questioning,
I saw people meeting eye to eye and standing
Half amazed by each other's presence
I saw their mouths silently shaping the word *why*
Why didn't we know this? and yet knowing
They already knew, and without words
We all stood searching for the gesture
That would say it –

As the lights went green, and we drove on.

Putney Bridge, London. April 1987.

SOUL BUSINESS

It's not a question of you and I now
It's what's really between us –
I said it's like being in another room
Or the same room, with all the lights turned out
Or underwater, holding your breath
As you float in front of me with your eyes closed

It's soul business now, and not what we have known
Or can claim from each other, or demand
That's over now, and the business I have with you
Is no business I can explain to anyone
And isn't your business maybe, either –

And what did I say? We are like wrong-footed dancers
As soon as I think it's *this* way, it reverses
By way of saying look, you don't know what it is
So would you mind just tripping over this puddle…
And I get up with my face muddied, humbled, laughing –

And look, don't give me neat words on paper
Speak it in the moment, breathe it, give it away
This stuff is for sharing out loud as it comes
As the best we can say – cracking it,
Silencing the crackling down the line…

Until we are one stream with cliff-path and sky
And each other, in the rain, or whatever the weather
We are one another, and it's the one plunge
That finds us together, here, all as friends

And lovers, where the wedding we are waiting for is all of us.

NAKEDNESS

for Alan Rycroft

Take off your robes, your cassocks, your regalia
You thought, as they swarmed in the auditorium
Shaven heads, saris, dhotis, shawls...
At the interfaith gathering in Calcutta –
And there were 'so many words', you said
There was the woman who stood up from the floor
And talked on and on about the I that is Thou
That is We that is me that is I, or something like that,
As you smiled and ached at her convolutions;
And then there was the rabbi who claimed
'My people are the saddhus of the world'
(My people, not yours): and for all this
Backscratching and talk of union
The same old secret pride and division

And who were you? What could you be then?
A nothing, a nakedness with no name but your own,
As you went to climb those steps bare-headed in the sun
High on a mountain above the village below
Where you sweated to the truth you found at the cave's mouth:

And what did you find? In its twilight depth
But the face of a friend that wore his face, and yours,
His, and yet yours – this Buddha
In his carved cool grey stone where you saw
He was no deity, but what we've made him:

He was human, and nakedly – that's what he'd achieved
As the straightjacket we'd given him crumbled away
And then you saw him as he saw you:

Your two faces, your bodies blending
In naked grey stone and naked flesh
Naked, face to face

In the word that is silence, breath and love,
And no pretence.

NEW LABOUR

with thanks to Dusty

We've solved the problem of the unemployed:
They're washing supermarket trays
For eight hour shifts with one fifteen minute break.

First day you said you were so knackered
You didn't know what to do with yourself.
A company director reduced to this –
Kitchen work, raking the ashes in hell.

Then there was the day when you did twelve hours
Because you had to clear food three weeks past its sell-by date.
Not even the flies would go near it.

One week of it – that's all you had, mercifully
And yet these guys were willing to do it day in, day out
For £4.50 an hour. Willing ? Do they have a choice ?

And did you talk? Oh no, there wasn't time for that.
It was literally non-stop. You had to keep going.
If I'd have had half an hour, my muscles would have seized up
– you added.

Two weeks later you could be in heaven
Reading meters for Severn Trent Water.
The boss back there said you'd be welcome anytime.

We've solved the problem of the unemployed:
They're washing supermarket trays
For eight hour shifts with one fifteen minute break.

A Tree I Know

for Mario Petrucci

It stands in the dream by the gate to the fields
Its leaves full of whispering particles of wind
Where every leaf is an unwritten poem of air
Unopened, in its spell of hush

In sunlight or moonlight, shimmering in the dark...

And how can we fix it, paint, or name it?
It holds us, as it holds the sea

In its mystery that is other, like you
With its broken mirror of leaves
I can't see myself in

So then it is a door – to the night or the day
Where our other voice speaks from inside the mist
And the sun, that is clarity to us

'I can only call it grace', you are saying

Where we can talk back
– and, who knows, to each other in the silence
Without even knowing –

At our separate desks, joined in the invisible skein of the air
Where we watch and pray.

And its leaves fill with seething air
Like an affirmation
Beyond the ending

As our eyes meet, pupil to pupil
Beyond the mere words we exchange

When You Find Yourself Strange
in the Eyes of the World

Take yourself in hand
Like this rare sunset sky all around you
As it touches you
In the round of its vast translucent membrane

Knowing you are as fragile
Transient and unique
As its fading amazing crimson-streaked expanse –

And that as you honour it
All that is outside you
Is within you

You are the one you came into the world to be

You are the one who is older now, and yet never is
You are the one who is different and yet always the same
And where the light in your eyes and your heart
Come, from far away

You are one who is beautiful
Before language or name

FROM GABRIEL'S ANGEL

for Gabriel Bradford Millar

Love is a wild thing
When we try
To tame it –

It is the tip of an eagle's wing,
Seen soaring –

A house without walls,
A messenger without flesh –

It is a very given thing
Where the giver
Is the astonished receiver –

And it is in her hands
Though she cannot see it…

It is the free communion
Between souls
That have chosen to breathe,

And are chosen
To bring the sky down
To the edges of their mouths and eyes

Knowing that paradise
Is not a place, or a name
But an infusion of the living air –

Where we are mortal and eternal
As we are man and woman
Haunted by where
We came from

That we have
To keep aspiring to –

Following that star
That crowns us
Across the sea

Of the dark
Occluded horizon…

Kosovo

The hollowed heart of Europe
Clenched like a fist

That one man – like a steel bullet –
Can break so many hearts

And we must stop him
Stop this

– stop what?

The one crime we can commit
To fail to recognise
That everything is our sister and brother,
And then to kill it

Till the world shrinks
To the size of our insignificance
– a polluted irritant in the eye of God –

A dream down the wrong end of a telescope
Becomes our fashionable fragmented nightmare

And it's only by filling our hearts up from the inside
With love and rage

That we can say No – or Yes – loudly enough
To see our world whole again.

Improvised on tape, driving.

ALWAYS AND ONLY THERE IS YOU, LIKE THE SKY OVER OUR HEADS, HIGHER THAN THE FURTHEST STAR, AND CLOSER TO US THAN OUR OWN BREATH IN OUR HEART OF HEARTS;

WE MUST RETURN TO YOU AGAIN.

AND ALWAYS, WE ARE ALONE, EACH ONE OF US, IN THE SECRET WOMB OF OUR LIVES WHERE WE GROW, JOURNEY AND DIE AND ARE CALLED TO STAND IN OUR OWN LIGHT;

WE MUST STAND AS WE ARE AGAIN.

AND AS LOVE IS THE WAY, MADE THROUGH THIS OPENING OF OUR HEARTS, THE ONE WE LOVE AND CHERISH WITH OUR HANDS IS THE MOST INTIMATE MIRROR OF WHO WE TRULY ARE;

WE MUST RETURN TO LOVE AGAIN.

AND ALWAYS, THOSE AROUND US AND WITHIN US, NEAR AND FAR, ARE THE FAMILY WE ARE CALLED TO BE A PART OF, TO NURTURE, FEED, AND SUSTAIN, AND TO LOVE AS WE ARE LOVED;

WE MUST MAKE LOVE ABUNDANT.

AND THROUGH THIS, IN ONE SMALL STEP, WE CAN SEE OUR EARTH AGAIN IN ALL ITS SPREADING CURVES OF LAND AND SEA, WITH ALL ITS FIELDS AND TREES, PEOPLES AND CREATURES, POISED IN THE OCEAN OF TIME…AND WE CAN SAY;

"THIS IS OUR GARDEN, AND IT IS OURS TO SERVE AS WE STAND IN YOU."

RAHEEN

for Virginia

Don't put the faith you have for God in people
You were told, walking in the woods above here.
It may be true. Let's say it is. And if you don't
What do you do with it ?

'Love one another' is the mystery
Because it means in spite of everything
It is the holes in the clouds we fall through
Like angels, back to earth.

It is the faith I have in God *in you*
That is the question.

Raheen is a hamlet near Piltown, Co. Waterford.

After Rumi I

for S.

Of course we tell each other everything,
That's what lovers are supposed to do.

Can we make a blossoming
With only one pair of hands?

The pearl we are has to be cracked open,
Before it becomes a pearl.

Don't fear your mouth
There's nothing to lose,
Only the cage of your unspeaking…

These words you are brought to
Are another kind of river –

The sweet water that wants
To flow through you like fire.

AFTER RUMI II

When he gets to the other side
He dances a song of ecstasy and praise with his whole body!

He can't believe what he sees –
The whole universe turned inside out from the heart all around him!

He flings his arms open wide –
Releasing the chains from inside each cell of him…

And do we have to wait till we die?
Will that be our greatest regret?
That we never knew *life*?

Back here, we grow older in boxes
Psychologically aware, in our stylish boxes

While what he says is
If you haven't learnt to praise and dance
The whole of your inner being stays closed like a door –

And you might as well have learnt nothing at all.

After Rumi V

Occluded sun –
Over the misty rain hills

This is Your Light
Like a candle in the depths

Saying *the clouds of the visible world*
Are our own –

And the ones we need
To find each other

And You within us
Where no sun shines

As what we know
Rises in our blood

Mirrored
In every act of love

Part of the Greater World
We cannot see:

Strange, to have eyes –
Yet to have none.

After Rumi IX

You can say what you like –
It isn't necessarily what you feel

You can name what you aspire to,
But it isn't what you practise.

Language is an elephant,
An emperor, a hollow reed...

Find the words that are your own
Fired from inside your skin

And from the place where you had nothing
But broken husks and shells of meaning

Then when you speak
You will say what you mean.

After reading an interview with the Poet Laureate in *ES* magazine

FOLLOW YOUR HEART

for P.

And there it was –
suddenly up ahead on the road
written in red all over the back of a yellow Walls lorry

An ice-cream heart
with a human one pounding behind
melting all time away…

And he was going some –
I had to put my foot down to keep up
as he swung round each bend in front of me

There was no getting past him
as the double central white lines also decreed

And it was my birthday
I was born and reborn
I was alive, and loving you
– what better present?

And I can tell you
it was great following my heart
there was nothing else left for me to choose

my fear slipped away,
I had enough to eat and breathe,
and though people complained
no one stood in the way of the wind –

the only unsafe thing was trying to photograph it…
that's the only moment I nearly came unstuck
when my front left tyre jumped the kerb

but still I did it – three times –
because when you follow your heart
that's exactly the kind of stupid thing you have to do.

Sixty Seconds in Alabama

OK: so you've got him in your rage-sight,
You've wrestled her down to darkness
But wait a minute: consider

You're about to pass sentence on yourself
And you'll never be able to escape.

You? Let's get this straight

This is not you: it is an entity,
A cancer that is ruining your life.

Don't care, you say. *Don't feel a thing*: you will
The knife you raise will slice through your heart
The trigger you pull will explode as many times
Until you see you're firing into a mirror

What is this? It's suicide.
And inside?
Even now

A numb voice crying out for love
Slapped down until you silenced it, too –
Now your rage is a wall no one can get through.

I want to get through to you.
I've been wanting to for a long time
But I can't unless you STOP.

Will you try? Just this:

Take your hand in your other hand.
Hold it still for a second. Feel it close,
Feel its warmth –
Palm to palm

Feel it speaking.
Wanting to live?
                    And maybe

Emergency, it says. Unbearable, yes –

So make that phonecall instead.

OTHERWISE

It has to be love
otherwise
we have come this far and it means nothing

it collapses like the rubble
of a shelled-out building,
and turns into its Anti-Christ –

a safe self-righteous order that is dead
that stands like two upended coffins
(that opens its eyes but closes its heart)

where love
to be love
to find itself as love again
always yearns to go that extra mile...

So as you drive now
listening to music that was silenced
that you self-silenced
it all floods back –

is your passion

and a road that's going Somewhere

as the whole day becomes a quiet celebration
of what it is, among smiles
and shining eyes...

And then, it is this crimson sky
　　in its broad brushed bands
　　　　you chase to see round the corner

it's walking in these twilight woods
　　where the sky beyond the silhouetted trees
　　　　is white and gold

it is the day's end that reaches
　　　　　　　　　　to the other side of the world

ALREADY THERE AT THE CENTRE

for Claire Knifton-Russell

There is a kind of flame that is in us that is deeper than our eyes,
than our hearts even, and that burns in spite of us, and which we
touch each other with and in – despite looking away, laughing, or
withdrawing in embarrassed incomprehension.

We touch each other with who we are, and we are touched by who
we are.

So we're sitting here now in this circle, in this dream tent, on this
particular piece of living ground.

This is what we've come to, in this facing one another, with our
eyes closed or open, even as we imagine it passing.

This is what we are doing here together, in this family with its many
faces – and alone as we are, in this silence we know we are not
separate: that was the great illusion, the untruth that crucified us
all – even as we each had to die in it.

And yet we will leave, and then?

Do I need to see you to be with you? Even as the air threatens to
tear skin?

Could I bear the ending of this longing ?

And the truth is, it breathes between us exactly as it needs to,
whatever we think we know or feel: as one place, one face gives
way to another, as we move and are moved in the measure of its
immeasurable dance.

And then, wherever we are we are already in the centre, and in the
centre of what it means to live the heart of our lives.

So come, lovers, friends, brothers and sisters, enemies become
pilgrims of truth –

This is our kingdom, and we have work to do.

Epiphany 2001

FOR THIS GENERATION

What a weight we've given you
Oceans, forests, mountains and rivers
Polluted and maimed – a world-weight,
And then to see the frame that holds it gone rotten
That we never had to recognize –

But most of all, you've been denied the Dream
By those whose soulless awakening
Denies it, and whose void is violence,
And you know (as we do) that without it
There is nothing worth waking for

So you must find it, as we each have to
With or without an understanding mother –
You must dare the adventure you will always remember
That moves your heart into your eyes as you think of it,

But dare it into life, please, stay with us
We need you here for the dream that never fades
Where we make Heaven on Earth as it was meant to be
And which only can be when we land inside ourselves,

Our souls shining out of each other's faces
As we put our shoulders to the wheel of day,
To heal our lover that is this wasted place –
As her arms reach out becoming trees, fields, towns, the sunset
And dawn horizon.

'Teach us how to remain'.

ANYTOWN, STROUD: TO YOU

The air suddenly warmer as you walk out, leaving your sanctuary
the lights of the town glittering, valley-cradled below –
the moon full, cloud-clear – and the sky a lustrous darkening blue,
as you climb the road passing the lit insides of the houses...
and the woman in the late shop unusually smiles –
and a man on your way back winds down his window
grateful to be shown the way

You lift your eyes again to the hills and their rising wooded edges
and where the land falls beyond to the river and the sea
and the place is a jewel, like this moment –
you can breathe...

A chance conversation with a neighbour completes it
enough to go back inside, and continue.

Don't believe every blue evening
but if you don't, what is there to believe in?

How else could your eyes reach
the miracle of another's in the dome of their sky?

And how would you ever dare to meet
this ebbing sea of air reaching your feet,

How could you ever call yourself happy,
or even feel you might be about to be?

Dream on, we need you – we all need you.

FOR EVERYTHING THAT LIVES IS HOLY

You have to choose: an animal is either an *it*,
Or a sentient being – it can't be both –
And if you choose death, that's all you are doing,
Killing yourself, saying what you're worth
(About as much meat, fit for cremation).
But choose life, and what would that be like?
It is the soul that comes out of your eyes
That comes back to meet you in theirs
That makes you a shepherd, so that no one
Has the right to rule your flock, only you
In the cloak you wear – and even with death
You have the power to love and bless
For everything that lives is holy, you've heard it said*
Which means we build Jerusalem here
In the centre of our heartbreak, brick by brick
Against everything that disconnects
Where we are the sickness and the cure,
And new life bleats half-heard inside us, in the wind.

---

*after William Blake

How

How do you know that the earth is yours?
Because it rises up under your feet

How do you know that the wind is yours?
Because it freshens a trace
Deep inside your breathing

How do you know what you see is yours?
Because your eyes rest
On its meniscus made of the clearest tears

How do you know that what you hear is yours?
Because it rinses all the channels
Of your being

How do you know that what you touch is yours?
Because it claims your body as its own

How do you know that what you taste is yours?
Because its bitterness gives way to water

How do you know that your voice is yours?
Because it insists on the secret of your becoming

How do you know that your name is yours?
Because it rings from heaven
Inside the skin of your heart

Improvised on tape, walking the cliff path towards George's Head, Kilkee, Co. Clare.

NIGRET

SACRED HEART: the ceramic house plaque says
and then, only a few yards down
behind the slit of a grey metal
sliding garage door
a topless blonde with unzipped jeans
stencilled in black on a pick-up's polished steel bumper,
its owner lurking in the shadows…

So what is sacred?
Mary, as she raises her eyes
out of a cornice high on a villa's veranda?
Two old nuns carrying a cardboard tray of veggies between them
stout as the salt of the ground?

The question hangs like an empty mouth

When out of nowhere, or perhaps the future,
appears a battered blue dust-streaked Cortina
big white letters emblazoned on its rear window
like solidified cloud

POWER
OF
LOVE

it proclaims –

And the car, parked up beyond the communal refuse bin,
With its registration KAN, and (we hope) here to stay.

Nigret is a part of Zurrieq, Malta.

from IN-FLIGHT

for C.

.

At such moments like this, when you are as ill as you are
and all I have is a mobile phone with £1.50 of credit
and I'm down the tunnel ten feet from the aircraft hatch
all there is to say is surely not 'How are you?',
or 'I was just thinking of you – '

But to go direct to the centre where we long
to be touched
to the same ever-sharpening edge you have brought me
all my life to
since I was too young or old to know –

'I love you'.

   *

We live in a world
where things are not as they should be
but where the balding shaven red-headed man
serving the in-flight tea or coffee
can give out as much love as anyone
as he tirelessly moves from row to row
with his Indian colleague behind the trolley
with his little blue tray for pouring the coffee
and blue-to-the-horizon horizontal azure cup –

whether he always means it, or not.

   *

'Wow, Mama, look!' she says
5 or 6 years old in her pink top, her hair tied in a centre-plait
as the plane tilts and all the windows
are reflected in a moving line of dazzling morning light
and what does Mama say?

I don't know, but her little girl looks down
as if embarrassed, and in that moment
I say to her without words what becomes a prayer
Don't lose your sense of wonder for anyone

INNISFREE

A sudden dip at the last bend in the lane
down where the concrete pier juts out over the edge
and the wind draughts towards you over the incoming waves
as you stand, in a blast of cool mountain-driven air –

There it sits, realer than a dream,
the greenest of secrets unto itself –
apart from its little wooden jetty
that says, or seems to say, 'you can reach me'

But there's no boat in sight
and no one to even ask…

And this is how close, and how far
the peace is where you're connected
through and through

And if I can't sit here in peace,
where there's no means to cross
and nowhere to rest
but the uncut tangled verge

I'll never reach it

and nor, my friend, will you.

In Co. Sligo, after Yeats.

La Maison de Dieu

This is the Tarot card of now:
and it's not an image
of a lightning struck tower
with its falling masonry and figures
it is the thing itself
it is transposed into
as each plane strikes
turned into an oven from the inside
exploding in terrible flame
as the nightmare begins
and the faces appear at the windows
helpless, beyond reach...

You watched them falling

It is those who chose to die
in a clean plummeting of air
It's those who stood below
crushed by its tidal breaking
It is the face of a priest asleep
whose prayer fell from the sky
that move you

Not the tower, the towers
in their thousand feet of silver
shimmering, mercurial and inflated
Not the tower that was
the Babel of its own security
but the human lives it sacrificed

And what it is to be brought to its root
in these latter days, long foreseen
that is what has to crash
before we can live as one
universal people

All that has been built up
that has to fall
you know it
it's not the rhetoric of war
that can answer it...

Zealots gave their lives for it
and is it possible, you ask,
irate, American, as you are
as something else comes over your face
that they did this for love too
or if not love, for the truth?

A terrorist truth is not love
or love as we know it
but one thing is beyond dispute
the secret doorway this tower leads to
that is the end of all vanity
blown open forever now –
where flame and blood and water come streaming,
it is the heart of our world opening
that buckles with these buildings
and every other tower that remains
that can draw lightning

Not the spire vanishing into the blue
or where the muezzin calls at evening
and the dervish turns and turns
without holding on to anything...

But you, as you wander the darkening streets
dust still hanging in the smoke-thick air
without quite knowing
where you are going
or where all of this is leading

This is the Tarot card of now
held in anyone's fingers
in three and four dimensions all around us
and what it spells is GRAIL among the ruins.

17.9.01

ANGEL OF THE NORTH

Astonishing the air –
wings-up alert as if just landed
out of the invisible's so much greater realm

and yet rooted as only presence can be
dwarfing the small hill become its base
above bushes in their sunlit spring-yellowing blaze
set against blue sky on this postcard...

And then who are you, bird-man, with your faceless face
your wing-struts stretched as wide as a jumbo jet's –
and the androgynous line of your body
rippling into solid merged gale-withstanding feet
where the weathered steel becomes wood so nearly breathing?

In one pair of eyes, for as long as it takes
to begin to absorb the amaze of you, I want to say
you are more purely here than we may know
not only created and cast, winched and hefted, inch by inch
but as a Being in the guise of the earth
and all our folly you stand beyond, transforming it
in the standing shape of your vigil

– as the road swings, as the camera pans,
in the flight of any bird's wings, around you –

and not as crucifixion now, but witness
to the greater world you announce that never leaves us
however ridiculous we are
waiting and waiting for us to awaken
and scale the hill-mound's tiny distance to you, for always.

'Angel of the North', cast in weathered steel, is by sculptor Anthony Gormley and stands beside the A1 near Gateshead in the North of England.

UNHOLY NIGHTS

And now we have no idea what's going on.

A country ringed by desert and darkness,
as it briefly parts –
revealing parachutists dropping towards a trench
as if landing on the surface of the moon.
No sound.

If you want to know about the war, ask us
says the Pentagon, and we will assure you
that collateral damage is as minimal as it's inevitable…
you saw those food parcels being dropped?
Good, keep looking at them.

Meanwhile we sit here and we know
what it is to be in truth with each other
it's the difference between posturing and a warm lingering kiss
flooding the lower body with moisture and blood

gazing into your clear exquisite eyes, and seeing them
under the candour of your eyebrows and your mouth.
And it's what you have when you've lost everything
so you can only begin again
when there's nowhere further to go down

And we know what it is to keep penetrating the mist
how easily it can reassume its place
and that telling the truth is not just once
but again and again as your stomach tightens
tempted to lie, knowing what the price is.

Meanwhile, this is no phoney war –
tomahawks blow bodies into offal in seconds
daubed around lunatic walls like excreta…
so don't be fooled by the velveteen silence

It's where we meet, with nothing to hold on to
only a stubborn flame of knowing in our guts
that is our most intimate song.

SELF-PORTRAIT

after the painting by Zdislaw Ruszkowski (c. 1967)

This is Modern Man:
diseased in the place of vision
his brow as if bared to the brain
– a whited cauliflower, with its stem
extending like a handle to the end of his nose...

Green about the gills, from the jacket to the neck
lime green like a grass stain, cheap green like disco light
and the face with its ambiguous pencilled moustache
and great open sad eyes, half in shadow
(hairline above receding into white)
that say it all: not mean at heart
only bemused by all he has seen
across a century of catastrophe –

and with the whole of his forehead
as if crying out for a hand of light

even as the sun seems to be brightening
from his own (is it? Could it be?)
invisible attending Self –
his spirit-level sight.

Abdul's Eyes

Like black suns...
                    and is it
because they seem too close together
– narrowed intense, unsmiling – or is it
just that they are long dark corridors of pain
that you can see every cruise missile flaring in,
every defaced mosque,

every pub or tube projection that says *suicide bomber
sleeping here among us?* Filling their onyx light
as you spread the samples on this small conference table
including one on Islamic Law, as your hands pause
spread briefly over its open pages
as its English breaks into bold curvaceous script
that is your otherness, and your courtesy –

and we smile at you, wanting to say 'friend'
and our light can't penetrate, as yours keep glancing away

then as you turn beside me again, the pain in yours
meets the fear in mine that is the fear in yours,
palpable as a glaucoma, its lenses glued on

until love can re-enter
dissolving them like the rain...

or in a soft single flash of unimagineable
shared laughter?

Like lightning, again?

PUBLIC ENEMY

Yours was the stone that slung
two terrified planes into Goliath's eye –
and one into his steel pentagram heart
the other bound for his white brain

But unlike David, this giant didn't die
and while one eye wept the other blazed
bringing back a firestorm of respite
to wreck yet more innocent lives...

Maybe it was because you were wrong
even in your rightness: that the end
could not justify the means
and that you could never be a king
(nor your fingers know the harp's bright strings)
while your goal was not healing, or peace

And because this is a giant you could never lay out
even with a hundred stones in your sling
a giant that says 'you are with us or against us'
a flag-waving giant that is raging in its sleep...

So all the more amazing that you should even try
knowing you could never win
that your victory could only be in defeat
that leaves your gesture pristine as it is:

knowing what it means to be no one's friend
strangely serving what we cannot see
framed from every angle to seem
as evil as we need you to be –

One man against everything the world has grown rotten in
wrong as it will always be, until we know we are one
family of suffering or love, in the end.

PRESENT MOMENT OF LOVE

I hold you and hold you and hold this
and suddenly
it doesn't matter anymore –

It matters supremely, and it doesn't

And because it's not a fantasy I want
an incorruptible bond, a future dream
when love is all around us here and now

Love is all around us when we let go
to the dance that is all of our faces –
in a circle as they move, in and out of view,
when we don't hold on

Even as we cherish each other to dying
as the circle takes us, now
and not in any way we've known;

And is this last threshold
before the dream can come true
or is it breaking the flask
before it's ready to be opened?

All we can know is how the mind becomes the heart
when all there is, is the present moment of love –
all there is, is you, and you, and you.

THE GOLDEN ROCK

Here on a sandy beach become a shelf of stone
as if placed by a huge deliberate hand
– rolled downhill in bone-crushing thunder –
this sand-gold boulder, like a giant full stop
with all the expanse of sunlit sea beyond
in this bay which means 'Little Garden'

As it hangs on its precipice, in far away Tibet
painted gold all over where it is poised forever;
and here it's mutable, airbrushed by wind and sun,
scored (as you come closer) with fig-sized circles
of vaginas, and graffitti names already fading
blurred, the oldest almost indecipherable
PALMILLA...and was it Toni, or Janice?
And the sand-covered face of a hooded alien
carved in laughter, become the ghost of a smile...

as cell by cell, rain wind and spray erase them
as from the surface of a mind, so that this rock
that could also be your anchorage
is constantly becoming where it came from
out of the high womb of the globingerinous cliff

golden as its gift to our eyes, and the sea.

Available from DAVID PAUL

Bland Ambition and other Poems by Michael Pierce

"These days my ambition/Extends to being at peace," explains Michael Pierce in the title poem. He draws on his Jewish roots, friendships, love of nature and the ups and downs of love to produce poetry that is tender, witty and stylish. His poems have been winners in national and regional competitions.

"Witty… beautifully honed… such quietly effective celebration calls to mind the joyful work of other Anglo-Jewish poets such as Bernard Kops and Dannie Abse" – Peter Lawson, *Jewish Chronicle*.

Coming soon…

Cutting Pomegranates by Miriam Halahmy

In *Cutting Pomegranates*, as in her first collection *Stir Crazy*, Miriam Halahmy invests everyday things with resonance. The pomegranate cut open reveals a bitterness of seeds, but also the promise of renewal, of new life.

"There are some poets whose voices ought to be heard urgently, such as Shelley and so is Miriam Halahmy." – John Rety.

Book With No Back Cover by Richard Burns

This collection brings together many of the poet's continuing preoccupations: the idea that no book is complete till a reader reads it; that the totality of any writer's *oeuvre* constitutes one work, one book; and the Biblical and mystical idea of the Book of Life. Richard Burns is the winner of numerous literary prizes.

"I am not a prophet but I believe you have written a great poem" – Octavio Paz on "Avebury."

"I believe Richard Burns will be one of the major poets writing in English in the early years of the new millennium… There is no other voice like his."– Anthony Rudolf.

To order these books, make cheques payable to:

David Paul, 29 Redston Road, London N8 7HL.

Bland Ambition £7.25 (£6 plus p&p)
Book With No Back Cover £9.50 (£7.99 plus p&p)
Cutting Pomegranates £9.50 (£7.99 plus p&p)

For more information call Dovidl Press tel. 020 8347 9857, or look at the website: **www.davidpaulbooks.com**